Threatened Wetlands

Catherine Chambers

CRABTREE
Publishing Company
www.crabtreebooks.com

Crabtree Publishing Company
www.crabtreebooks.com

Author:
Catherine Chambers

Editorial director:
Kathy Middleton

Proofreaders:
Crystal Sikkens, Molly Aloian

Designer:
Paul Myerscough

Production coordinator:
Kenneth Wright

Prepress technician:
Kenneth Wright

Illustrations:
Geoff Ward

Cover::
The beaver has often been blamed for flooding caused by the building of their dams. In fact, beaver dams provide a habitat for other wetland species, help to purify water, and actually slow the flow of floodwaters.

Photos:
Corbis: Earl & Nazima Kowall p. 23t, David Muench p. 18; FLPA: Roger Tidman p. 13; Getty Images: Peter Essick/Aurora p. 7t, Jacob Silberberg p. 17b; Istockphoto: Peter Malsbury p. 19t; Rex Features: p. 5t, Sipa Press p. 21t; Shutterstock: Vera Bogaerts p. 4-5, George Burba p. 7b, Joseph Calev p. 6, Tony Campbell p. 24–25, Sam D Cruz p. 15, FiremanYU p. 6–7, FloridaStock p. 5b, 10l, Steffen Foerster Photography p. 9t, 29, Filip Fuxa p. 24, Wong Yick Heng p. 14–15, Coia Hubert p. 26, Imageshunter p. 22-23, Iofoto p. 19b, Cynthia Kidwell p. 27t, Falk Kienas p. 12-13, Sebastian Knight p. 10–11, Rene Mattes/Hemis p. 21b, Jane McIlroy p. 17t, John Nguyen p. 8-9, Pix2go p. 27b, Melissa Schalke p. 1, 3, 18–19, 30–31, 32, Ljupco Smokovski p. 9b, Joy Stein p. 16-17, TebNad p. 20-21, Nikita Tiunov p. 25t, Paul S. Wolf p. 28–29, Worldpics p. 23b.

Cover photograph:
Shutterstock (Pix2go, Bruce Johnstone)

Library and Archives Canada Cataloguing in Publication

Chambers, Catherine, 1954-
    Threatened wetlands / Catherine Chambers.

(Protecting our planet)
Includes index.
ISBN 978-0-7787-5214-1 (bound).--ISBN 978-0-7787-5231-8 (pbk.)

    1. Wetlands--Juvenile literature. 2. Wetland ecology--Juvenile
literature. 3. Wetland conservation--Juvenile literature. 4.
Environmental
degradation--Juvenile literature. I. Title. II. Series: Protecting
our planet
(St. Catharines, Ont.)

QH541.5.M3C43 2010   j577.68'27   C2009-905231-8

Library of Congress Cataloging-in-Publication Data

Chambers, Catherine, 1954-
 Threatened wetlands / Catherine Chambers.
    p. cm. -- (Protecting our planet)
 Includes index.
ISBN 978-0-7787-5231-8 (pbk. : alk. paper) -- ISBN 978-0-7787-5214-1
(reinforced library binding : alk. paper)
1. Wetlands--Juvenile literature. 2. Wetland conservation--Juvenile
literature. I. Title. II. Series.

QH541.5.M3C43 2009
333.91'816--dc22

                                                    2009034867

Crabtree Publishing Company
www.crabtreebooks.com   1-800-387-7650

Published in Canada
Crabtree Publishing
616 Welland Ave.
St. Catharines, ON
L2M 5V6

Printed in China/122009/CT20090915

Published in the United States
Crabtree Publishing
PMB16A
350 Fifth Ave., 59th floor
New York, NY 10118

Published by CRABTREE PUBLISHING COMPANY.
Copyright © **2010**

Contents

What are wetlands?

Wetlands are habitats on and around shallow water, mud, or damp, spongy soils. They range from low coastal **saltmarshes** to high, upland freshwater **bogs**. Some shimmer in tropical heat, while others shiver in Arctic cold. Some are permanent while others are seasonal. None of them has water over 20 feet (six meters) deep.

Wildlife havens

Wetland habitats are full of wildlife, from reeds and water lilies to beavers and wading birds. Wetlands help control flooding. They also absorb **greenhouse gases** that are making Earth's atmosphere hotter. However, half the world's wetlands have been destroyed over the last 100 years, mostly through human activity and climate change.

"We lost in excess of 30 square miles [78 square km] of our coast just during the 36 hours of Hurricane Katrina and it will be very, very difficult to restore that coastline."

Carlton Dufrechan, Lake Pontchartrain Basin Foundation, Louisiana, USA

◄ *Wetland marshes in Finland provide a unique environment for wildlife.*

CASE STUDY

Gulf Coast wetland disaster

On August 29, 2005, Hurricane Katrina shattered America's southern Gulf Coast. It killed at least 1,836 people and also destroyed thousands of buildings across the state of Louisiana. Damaged coastal wetland was partly responsible for the impact of the **hurricane**. This coastline has 3.5 million acres (1.4 million hectares) of marsh and **swamp**. These areas act as a buffer between the sea and inland areas. This is because hurricanes slow down when they hit the shallow wetland waters, leaving behind the warm, deep sea that fuels them. The Gulf wetlands have been **eroded**, or worn away, so the region's defense against storms has been reduced. In the last 75 years over 1900 square miles (5,000 square kilometers) have been lost.

Wetlands around this region include wooded swamps, sandy barrier islands,

▲ *Weakened wetlands on the Gulf Coast could not hold back Hurricane Katrina, and coastal waters swept inland.*

and grassy marshland that can be salty, slightly salty, or fresh water. These wetlands have shrunk because the Mississippi River that fed them with water and **sediment** has been blocked off by huge man-made banks called levees. Wetland areas have also been destroyed by thousands of miles of dredged channels. These have been dug out for shipping and oil pipelines. The channels have allowed saltwater to flow into freshwater wetlands. The salt has killed wetland forests, such as the **cypress** swamps. The roots of these and other woody plants once bound the wet soil together. For many years, these soils have been eroded, reducing the wetland buffer zone.

◄ *Herons, such as this great white egret, thrive in wetland habitats.*

Where are wetlands?

Wetlands can be saltmarshes, inland freshwater marshes, **peat** land, and bogs. They include inland river **deltas**, and coastal deltas where a river meets the sea. Swamps, lakes, desert **oases**, flat river **floodplains** and even your local dam, pond, or ditch, are all wetlands, too. Most wetlands are natural while some have been made artificially.

Wetlands in the desert

Oases, and many shallow desert lakes and marshlands, occur above artesian aquifers. These are underground water reserves that have formed on top of impermeable rock, which does not let water drain through. Desert storms and seasonal rivers fill the aquifers. But sometimes, long periods without rain, called droughts, shrink the desert wetlands, such as those of Australia's Great Artesian Basin.

▼ *Wetlands can be found in both cold and warm climates. This wetland is in the sunny Yucatan Peninsula, Mexico.*

Wetlands in the ice and snow

Cold or frozen bogs and small **corrie lakes** are features of cold high plateaus and mountainous areas. Many of these types of wetlands were created when the last ice Age ended, over 10,000 years ago. During the Ice Age, gritty glaciers, or huge tongues of ice, grated against the underlying rock, scouring and scraping out dips. As the ice retreated, the dips were gradually filled with water and sediment, and plant life began to grow there. Siberia has bogland the size of France and Germany put together.

▲ *Wetlands are an important food source for fishermen in Lake Chad in Africa.*

Fact bank

Great wetlands of the world

Eurasia West Siberian Lowlands—Bogs and fens (low-lying marshes) over 1,060,000 square miles (2,745,000 square km).

South America Amazon River Basin Floodplain—Forest and savannah (grassy plains), **mangrove** and marshes over 672,000 square miles (1,740,000 square km).

North America Hudson Bay Lowland—Bogs, fens, swamps, and marshes over 144,000 square miles (374,000 square km).

Africa Congo River Basin—Swamps, wet grassland, and riverside forest over 73,000 square miles (190,000 square km).

Where the river slows down

Rivers are fast-flowing in upland areas but when they reach the river valley floor, they slow down. The river bed becomes wide and the waters overflow on either side of the river during heavy rain. It is here on the floodplain that vast wetlands spread out.

▼ *Siberian wetlands include many huge regions of bog and fenlands.*

7

Wonderful wetlands

Wetlands are wonderful for the natural environment. They help control water flow. They act as sponges, soaking up floodwater then slowly releasing it. This helps control **inundation** and coastal erosion. Wetlands also filter out excess **nutrients** found in agricultural fertilizers. These chemicals would otherwise pollute rivers and dams.

Regulating climate

Wetlands can regulate climate for an entire region, providing plenty of rain at the right time in the right amounts. This is because the Sun causes evaporation. This creates moisture in the air and rainclouds. Even small wetland areas help local moisture levels in this way. They create their own small microclimate, that is the unique climate of a small-scale area. This could be a garden pond or a larger body of water which cools the local atmosphere.

How are wetlands destroyed?

Increased human population has led to great demands on wetlands. They supply water to towns and cities, they are used as fishing grounds, for food production, and as waterways for boats.

◄ *Mosses and lichens grow in abundance on the Milford Track wetland in New Zealand.*

▲ *Wetlands are vital for the herds of migrating animals that gather at water holes in East Africa.*

Supplying water to towns and cities can drain a whole wetland during a very hot summer, leading to drought. This can mean that wetlands reduce in size considerably. In winter and spring, these smaller wetland areas lead to more flooding, as there are fewer wetland 'sponges' to soak up the water.

Many wetlands took thousands of years to form. Yet some are taking just weeks to be destroyed. Many wetlands are drained, filled in and built on, or they are used for grazing and agriculture. Other wetlands are starved of water and sediment when rivers are channeled for shipping or to stop the rivers flowing onto agricultural land or built-up areas.

Many anglers enjoy their favorite pastime of fishing in the wetlands. ➤

> "The world's wetlands, threatened by development, drainage, and climate change, could release a planet-warming 'carbon bomb' if they are destroyed."
>
> **Reuters News Agency reporting on a statement made by a science conference in Brazil, 20 July, 2008**

Wetlands and global warming

The destruction of wetlands is believed to contribute further to global warming. This is because wetlands hold a lot of carbon from decayed plant matter. They also absorb carbon dioxide, a greenhouse gas. Destruction of the wetlands causes carbon gas emissions, which lead to more global warming. However, healthy wetlands do release methane, which is another greenhouse gas, into the atmosphere through decaying vegetation, especially in warm weather. Scientists do not yet fully understand the role that wetlands play in the process of global warming.

Draining the wetlands

Humans have drained wetlands for hundreds of years, mainly for grazing, agriculture, and settlement. Today, they are also drained for roads, airports, and industry.

Wetlands without water

Draining the wetlands means a huge loss of wildlife habitat. It makes the wetlands' fine, silty soils become dusty and crumbly. This means they are easily eroded. The soil is blown or washed away. Drained wetland soils have greater concentrations of salts and acids. These poison native plant species, whose roots once bound the wetland soils together. The salts and acids can also stunt farm crops. Flooding from the sea or rivers is a constant threat to people living on reclaimed low-lying wetland areas.

▼ *Wading birds feed on frogs and fish in the shallow water of wetlands. If the wetlands disappear, so will their sources of food.*

▼ *Dikes, or mud banks, are a familiar sight in the countryside of much of the Netherlands. They were built to stop drained land from flooding.*

The polders of the Netherlands

A lot of the Netherlands lies on flat river delta land. Here, three of Europe's greatest rivers – the Rhine, Maas, and Waal – make their way slowly into the North Sea. This delta area is naturally wet and soggy. But in the Middle Ages, farmers and settlers began to dig ditches to drain away the water. They built banks called dikes to stop water from flooding back on to the drained land. The areas of land inside the dikes are called polders. These were used mainly to graze cattle. Farmers built mounds, called terps, to construct farmsteads and small villages above the drained land.

Wetland soils shrank without their supply of water and became lower than sea level. This meant that they could be flooded by the sea as well as the rivers. The windmill was used after this time to draw water out of the polders, keeping them dry. By 1852, steam pumping stations were used.

There have been many disasters on the polders. The worst occurred in February 1953, when a hurricane force wind and very high spring tides pushed seawater over the dikes, killing 1,835 people and 47,000 cattle.

▲ *This map of the Netherlands shows regions that are likely to flood.*

About 494,000 acres (200,000 ha) of land were flooded, and 3,000 homes and 300 farms were destroyed. It has taken over 40 years for the Netherlands' Delta Project to be completed. It included the building of enormous dams, and sluice gates that control water levels by opening and closing to let water in or out. However, in 1993 and 1995 these measures could not stop flooding from rivers that swelled through central Europe and on to the polder lands.

Dams and dredging

Dams are often constructed along the courses of rivers. They hold back and store huge amounts of water and silt that otherwise would have flowed or filtered through to wetland areas. This has led to the loss of wetland habitats. On the other hand, small dams have created wetland habitats, too. Dams are not the only way people have interfered with the flow of rivers.

Water highways

Rivers have been streamlined by levees, deep dredging for shipping, and canalling (making a canal). All these constructions have been made by humans. They have enabled rivers to run straighter and deeper. In turn, though, they have taken water away from their floodplains and deltas. They have also made the rivers flow faster.

▼ *Turning rivers into canals can harm local environments. Floodwater becomes diverted from natural wetlands.*

WHAT CAN BE DONE?

The River Danube flows for 1,770 miles (2,850 km) and its delta is the second-largest wetland area in Europe. However, the river has been dammed, canalled, and diverted for over 150 years by many of the ten countries that it touches. This has meant that there is less freshwater and silt flowing on to floodplains and the delta wetlands that fan out into the Black Sea. It has also meant that the Danube Delta's 5,000 animal species are under threat. Many of them rely on the wetland areas to breed, and the long, unbroken stretches of the river to feed.

The Danube Delta is home to more than 70 freshwater fish species and 300 bird species that include white pelicans, herons, egrets, spoonbills, and glossy ibises. In 1991, the Danube Delta was selected by UNESCO (United Nations Educational, Scientific and Cultural Organization) as a World Heritage Site, and by the WWF (World Wildlife Fund) as an important region for **biodiversity** conservation.

During a flood, water rushes down the channel and causes a flood at the end. Also, if the channel is just not deep enough, floodwater escapes over the top, submerging (covering with water) the surrounding land. Water can even breach (crack open) steep levees. Controlling the flow of rivers can damage wetland environments and wildlife, too. It starves them of freshwater.

The pygmy cormorant ➤ is an endangered species found on the Danube Delta.

Building on wetlands

Towns built on coasts are busy places, with activities such as trade, tourism, shipping, and industry. Many have grown so large that they now spill out on to coastal wetlands. Inland wetland areas are flat and often connected to **navigable** rivers. This makes them useful places to build on. However, building on wetlands has destroyed precious habitats.

Sinking and flooding

Whole cities such as London, New York, Chicago, and Washington all lie on top of drained wetland. So, too, do some airports and even nuclear energy plants. But building on wetlands is risky. In some areas, buildings have sunk into the fine, silty wetland soils. In other areas, there have been terrible floods.

"We need to face the reality that these floods are going to occur, and maybe the best solution is to move out of the way."

Erich Picha, Friends of the Earth (environment organization), 2007

In the United States, 17 million acres (seven million ha) of wetland have been built on, or ploughed up, in the Missouri and Mississippi river basins, and flooding is common.

▲ *In Cambodia, many people live in villages that float on the water.*

For this reason, in affected areas, many wetlands have been drained and built on. But wetlands may not be the real problem. In healthy, unpolluted wetlands, fish eat the **larvae** of the mosquito and keep their numbers under control. Pools of dirty, stagnant water, often without oxygen, away from the wetlands are more to blame.

Wetlands and the mosquito

Mosquitoes live near and breed on still, non-salty water, such as freshwater wetlands. Different mosquitoes can carry diseases, including malaria, dengue fever, yellow fever, Ross River virus, and West Nile virus. Malaria infects at least 500 million people every year and kills at least one million.

WHAT CAN BE DONE?

The American state of Massachusetts is determined to preserve its wetlands. The Massachusetts Department of Environmental Protection has connected computerized aerial maps to a database of wetland areas. It has discovered that 3,000 areas of wetland were built on without permission between 1991 and 2001. This data has helped the state to restore some wetland areas. It has also led to tighter local planning regulations to protect wetland areas. These prevent dredging, filling, and building on wetlands. They also forbid discharging pollutants into wetlands.

◄ *Cambodians depend on their boats to get around their floating villages.*

Power and the wetlands

Wetlands are polluted by spills from oil exploration. They are also bulldozed and burned so that palm oil can be grown, mainly for use as a **biofuel**. These activities are wiping out wetland habitats. They are also destroying the world's best **carbon sink** because wetlands absorb more harmful carbon gases than any other kind of habitat.

The price of oil

Oil exploration and oil spills from tankers threaten coastal wetlands in many parts of the world. In the Niger Delta, about 1.6 million tons (1.5 million tonnes) of oil has leaked into the wetlands over the last 50 years. The delta has many different wetland habitats—from its swamp forests and 6 mile (10 km) deep mangroves to its sandy barrier islands. The region's biodiversity is astonishing. It is home to a range of creatures, from the red Colobus monkey to the Heslop's pygmy hippo. However, the habitats of these creatures are being poisoned and suffocated by the oil.

▼ *Coastal mangrove swamps are often cut down to make charcoal, which is used as a fuel.*

CASE STUDY

The power of peat

Peat wetlands lock up vast amounts of the world's carbon gases. These are greenhouse gases that keep in heat and contribute to global warming. There are 988 million acres (400 million hectares) of peat wetlands in the world and they make up 40 percent of all wetlands. They are found from cold Alaska and Siberia, to temperate parts of Europe to tropical Indonesia. Peat is made from partially decayed plant matter, tiny leafy plants called mosses, and grasses, shrubs, and trees. It supports plants as tall as the 164 feet (50 m) ramin tree. Peat lands are home to many endangered species such as the Sumatran tiger and the estuarine crocodile.

But peat lands are in peril. In Indonesia, they are being burned and bulldozed in order to grow palm oil. This is used as a

▲ *The destruction and loss of vast peat wetlands contributes to global warming.*

biofuel instead of petroleum oil, and in foods and cosmetics. In the United Kingdom, peat was once dug up slowly by hand and burned as a fuel. Then it was scooped up by diggers and sold as a soil improver in garden centers. The United Kingdom has lost 172,200 acres (69,700 ha) in the last 50 years. The loss of peat across the world has contributed to global warming, which is thawing some of the massive frozen peat lands in Siberia. These are now releasing methane, another harmful greenhouse gas.

◄ *Pollution from towns in the Niger Delta is harming the area's wetlands.*

17

Wetlands tourism

Tourism brings a lot of money to local communities and governments. This is why many coastal wetland areas have been drained to supply water for vast hotel complexes, golf courses, swimming pools, and water sporting lakes.

The cost of coastal tourism

Other wetland areas have been filled in and hotels and golf courses built on top of them. Some wetlands have become **sewage** outlets for resorts, while others are clogged with litter. France, Italy, Spain, and Greece have already lost almost half of all their coastal wetland areas to tourism. It is estimated that by 2025, the Mediterranean coastal area will attract over 350 million tourists every year.

> "The tourism industry's growing demand for water-guzzling facilities and services, such as water parks, golf courses, and landscaping, is destroying the very resource it depends on."
>
> **Holger Schmid,
> World Wildlife Fund, 2004**

◄ *Many wetland areas in Florida have been built on to create water sites for tourists, such as water parks.*

CASE STUDY

The Okavango Delta

Wetlands make wonderful tourist destinations. For example, the Okavango Delta in Botswana, in central southern Africa, has about 50,000 visitors each year. The delta amazes wildlife tourists, photographers, and painters with its hippos, Nile crocodiles, sable antelopes, white rhinos, African fish eagles, and many other species. The delta is fed every year by wet-season rains that swell the Okavango River. Its waters cascade into the delta, creating Lake Ngami at its southern tip. The Botswana government planned to drain some of the delta for agriculture, but then they decided to keep it mainly as a wildlife haven. In 1996 the Okavango Delta was

▲ *Hippos and other wildlife attract many tourists to Botswana's Okavango Delta.*

made into a Wetland of International Significance by the Ramsar Convention— the leading wetlands organization in the world. However, the threat of too many tourists and hotels is never far away. Together with global warming and grazing, these threats have shrunk the delta to half its original size. At its peak, the Okavango Delta was once about 21,000 square miles (55,000 square km).

▼ *This wetland area in North Carolina is being used for boating activities. This harms the wetland and its wildlife.*

War and the wetlands

War has caused the destruction of natural habitats and agricultural land for thousands of years. When wetland habitats are destroyed, they take a very long time to recover. Sometimes they never recover. This is because once water has been drained or poisoned, wetland plants die and their roots no longer hold the wetland together.

Waging war on wetlands

During human conflict, wetlands suffer from destruction by tanks, land mines, and trenches. They can be poisoned by chemicals. Armies may deliberately destroy food sources for local people such land flooded to plant rice called rice paddies.

Parts of the Mekong Delta in Asia are still suffering from effects of the Vietnam War (1959–1975). Five million acres (two million ha) of wetland were drained.

▼ *Bombs dropped from war planes during times of conflict can devastate wetland areas and the wildlife that lives there.*

Iraq's Marsh Arabs lead a traditional way of life. They live in houses built of reeds.

> "When I can do a kayak trip from Baghdad all the way to Chibaish passing through the restored marshes, then I will consider myself done [with the restoration]."
>
> **Dr Azzam Alwash, Director, Eden Again Project**

Some were bulldozed or destroyed with high explosives. Over 37,000 acres (15,000 ha) of mangrove forest was destroyed by herbicides. Cape Camau lost up to 50 percent of its productive wetland woodland and fisheries.

The Mekong Delta has not fully recovered from the Vietnam War. Vital mangrove swamps, waterways, and fertile paddy fields were destroyed by bombing during the war.

WHAT CAN BE DONE?

Iraq's southern marshlands once covered 8,000 square miles (21,000 sq km) and were called the "Garden of Eden." But when the Marsh Arabs rose against Iraq's ruler, Saddam Hussein, in 1991, he responded by killing them. Many fled to save their lives. Then Saddam Hussein began to destroy the marshlands by diverting and damming water from the Tigris and Euphrates rivers. Canal links were destroyed, reed beds were burned, and many areas were poisoned. When Saddam's regime fell, some Marsh Arabs began to return to the area and breached dam and canal walls to flood the wetlands again. About 40 percent were inundated, although not all habitats have recovered well. Since then, the Eden Again Project is restoring the wetlands. It could take until 2014 to achieve its goals.

Polluting the wetlands

Poor sanitation and chemical pollution from industry and agriculture are threatening all types of wetland, from coastal **estuaries** to inland lakes. The pressure of the world's growing population is adding to both problems.

Waste and the wetlands

Factories use wetland waters in the manufacturing process. They discharge their industrial waste into them, too. This waste can contain bleaches used in paper-making, or poisonous mercury, chromium, lead, and cadmium metals. In humans, these can cause brain disorders, some cancers, and even death. Wetland plants are good at absorbing chemicals, but they can only cope with a certain amount of poison.

Air pollution affects wetland animals and is absorbed through plant leaves. Cement and chemical fertilizer plants in particular can pollute the air with the gas sulphur dioxide. Wetlands also soak up fertilizer chemicals, such as nitrogens and phosphates, through **runoff** from agricultural fields.

▼ *Wetlands are under threat from the quantity of waste dumped in them.*

Pesticides containing the poison cyanide have also been found in wetlands. Many of these chemicals are banned, but they still linger in the wetlands. So, too, do mountains of garbage, especially plastics.

Pollution threatens the people who depend on rice paddies for food. ➤

CASE STUDY

Pollution in the rice paddies

Some of the most polluted wetlands are artificial rice paddies, which are valuable wetland habitats. Rice paddies are mostly seasonal, controlled wetlands. They are habitats for an amazing range of wildlife. They provide all kinds of food for humans, too. In just one small area of Java Island, in Indonesia, research showed that 26 fish species swam and fed in the paddy; 17 of these were eaten by local rice growers, who farmed some of them. There were also five amphibian species, two reptile, two prawn, four mollusk, and ten aquatic plant species. Many of the leaves of these rice plants are cooked by the rice-growers, too.

However, pollution from poor sanitation, and metal poisons from industry are threatening rice-growers' health and the lives of wetland species in many parts of the world. So scientists are developing **GM** (Genetically Modified) varieties of rice that resist absorbing metals and toxins such as arsenic, which can cause cancer. This could help restore confidence in rice and will help save the paddy. But other species in this wetland habitat will still be threatened by polluted **groundwater**. Many rice growers are trying to tackle the pollution itself, especially chemical pollution from fertilizers and pesticides.

A huge variety of wildlife, such as these Balinese ducks, exists in the rice paddies of Bali, Indonesia. ➤

Plants in danger

Wetland habitats are home to many species of plant and plant-like organisms. Wetland plant life provides food, shelter, and breeding grounds for species of insects, fish, birds, amphibians, reptiles, and mammals. The plants absorb pollutants such as nitrogens and phosphates from farm fertilizers, too.

A world of wetland plants

Wetland plants range from tiny plant-like **algae**, to beautiful lilies and grassy sedges, to trees that grow to over 118 feet (36 m) tall. They grow in soils that range from damp peat and sand to saturated, or soaked, layers of decayed plant matter.

Cold and often frozen bogs are very flat, but are rich in soft mosses. They are home, too, to lichens, which make very good food for reindeer.

Wetland forests have trees at least 20 feet (6 m) tall. They range from conifers such as spruce and fir in cold climates, to species of oak in temperate zones. Wetlands in tropical zones have a huge range of plants, from mangrove forest to tall rainforest species that shelter many endangered animals such as the orangutan in Borneo and Sumatra.

Threats to wetland plants

Clearing and draining land are the greatest threats to wetland plants. This can be the result of agriculture or building. Cutting or tearing up wetland plants exposes their roots. The plants are then unable to absorb pollutants.

◀ *Wet meadows include many species of rushes, reeds, and sedges.*

▲ *Exotic plants like water hyacinths can soon become invasive species.*

Many native wetland plants will die. Waters rich in fertilizer runoff from farms are perfect for dense blankets of blue-green algae that take oxygen from the water and starve even more wetland plants beneath. Native wetland species are also being threatened by **invasive** species. These competing plant species were introduced from other parts of the world, often as ornamental plants.

WHAT CAN BE DONE?

Water hyacinth species are native to South America and they have been introduced to North America, Australia, and many parts of Asia as beautiful aquatic garden plants. But they have been allowed to spread out into the wild. Here, they are pushing out native wetland species. Fertilizer use is being reduced to help contain the water hyacinth. A species of weevil that eats into the hyacinth and kills it is also helping. In North America, the European species of a common water reed is rapidly pushing out the native reed. Cutting, burning, and smothering the invasive water reed with plastic to cut out sunlight are all helping to win the battle to protect the native water reed.

▼ *Water lilies are hardy swamp plants. They can survive on the water's surface where*

Animals in danger

Thousands of animal species live in wetlands. Wetlands are welcome stopping points for many other species. In the United States, 85 percent of all wild animal species depend on wetlands. Yet wetland animals are threatened constantly by loss of habitat and pollution. Others are poached for their fur or for the pet market.

Wetland creatures

Wetland animals live on, in, or by the side of wetland habitats. Species range from bristly water-worms and darting water beetles, to damselflies and dragonflies, to fish, muskrats, mink, and beaver. There are owls, booming bitterns, and bright blue indigo buntings. Wasp spiders and crab spiders live in the wetlands along with frogs, newts, toads, and snakes. Browsing reindeer and grazing buffalo rely on wetlands. Some species of monkey depend on them, too, as well as apes such as the orangutan.

▼ *Beavers construct their dams with branches, twigs, moss, and mud.*

Beaver dams

Some wetland animals, such as the beaver, have been misunderstood. The beaver has been hunted not only for its fur but also because it has been blamed for building dams that cause floods. Dams are built by beavers to create a wetland habitat and home for their families. These dams provide a habitat for other wetland species, too. They also purify the water and actually slow floodwaters.

Dangers of introduced species

Not all creatures are welcome in the wetlands. One unwanted rodent is the South American coypu, which has found its way into the United States. In Chesapeake Bay, this little creature is eating at the roots of wetland plants. The plants create a root mat that holds wetland soils together, so the coypu is destroying the foundation of the habitat.

▲ Amphibians such as toads and frogs thrive in wetland habitats.

WHAT CAN BE DONE?

There are many projects worldwide to help wetland species survive. One of these was set up in 1997 to protect the West Indian whistling duck, which is one of the rarest ducks in the Americas. The program concentrates on conserving wetlands where they live and encouraging local people to observe and count them. Education has stopped people from taking the birds' eggs and from hunting them.

◄ Beavers can carry materials for their dams with their forepaws and mouths.

27

Protecting our planet

Healthy wetlands can help save Earth. If wetlands are not smothered by pollutants, their plants and soils can help purify our planet. Wetlands can absorb unwanted carbon gases and offset the effects of global warming. They can soak up rising seawaters and can help stop coastal erosion, too. But how can we help save them?

Wetlands crisis talks

In 1971, a conference on the world's wetlands took place in Ramsar, Iran. It alerted the world to the importance of wetlands to our planet. At first, it was mostly concerned with the problems of wetland birds. But since then, the organization, now known as Ramsar, has supported all kinds of wetland projects. It now has 152 member nations. Over 1,675 wetland areas are protected or managed in a sustainable way for the people who live on them. Ramsar works with other organizations to achieve this, such as UNEP (United Nations Environmental Program).

▼ *Brazos Bend State Park in Texas has a variety of wildlife, from water lilies to snakes and alligators.*

▲ *A favorite wetland species is the lesser flamingo, which flocks in great numbers.*

"Many may be unaware that wetlands are disappearing faster than rainforests and over the last century half of the world's wetlands have been lost. But they are vital to our communities."

Liz Lamb, journalist, Newcastle, United Kingdom

Warfare and economic pressures are threats to the progress of wetland habitats. Climate change and the lack of cooperation between nations that own headwaters that feed wetlands are also concerns. These will all test the plans of Ramsar and UNEP's World Conservation Monitoring Centre.

HOW CAN WE PROTECT OUR PLANET?

We can all be involved in helping to save wetlands.

- Identify local wetlands, even small ones such as local ponds. With your friends, family, and school try to keep them healthy for wildlife.

- Put together a team to monitor the wetland—its health and wildlife. Identify species and keep track of them.

- Reduce your use of chemicals, especially detergents, by using bio-friendly alternatives.

- Keep the wetland free of unwanted weeds and litter.

- Do not use plastic bags. There are many reusable bags made of renewable materials such as hessian.

- Think about where you go on vacation. Will this have a negative impact on wetland habitats?

- Are there alternatives to your usual vacation? Find out about working vacations that help to preserve wetlands, or local projects you could join.

Glossary

alga (plural, algae) A tiny water plant

biodiversity Range of Life

biofuel A fuel made from crops

bog Damp ground made of peat soils

carbon sink Something that absorbs carbon dioxide, preventing too much of the gas entering the atmosphere

corrie lakes Land scoured out by glaciers, which fills with water

cypress A conifer tree that grows in swamp forests

delta A low-lying, swampy plain where a river flows into a sea or inland lake

erode To wear away

estuary A marshy area near a sea or lake, where a river slows down

floodplain Flat land on either side of a river. Flooding deposits silt here

GM (Genetically Modified) Plants or animals that have been altered by changing the chemical instructions that make them grow

greenhouse gases Gases such as carbon dioxide that create a band around Earth, trapping in heat

groundwater A water source under the ground

hurricane A fierce storm that develops over large bodies of water and hits land

inundation A flood that sweeps in over land

invasive Having a tendency to spread into native species and plantlife

larva (plural, larvae) A small, worm-like stage in the life cycle of many insects

mangrove A tree with twisting roots that grows in muddy coastal swamps

navigable A stretch of water that is easily used by boats

nutrients Chemicals that help plants to grow

oases Areas of water within desert around which plants grow

peat Damp soil made from deep, partly decayed plant matter

pesticides Chemicals used to prevent pests, such as insects, from eating crops

runoff Excess water used to irrigate farmland, which runs off the farmland and into surrounding areas

saltmarsh Wet, salty land on the coast or inland salt lake or sea

sediment Fine soils and rock fragments carried in a body of water

sewage Waste water from homes and industry

swamp Low, waterlogged land

Further information

Books

Wetlands in Danger by Andrew Campbell (Franklin Watts, 2005)

Wetlands by Robert Snedden (Franklin Watts, 2004)

What are Wetlands? (The Science of Living Things), by Bobbie Kalman and Amanda Bishop (Crabtree, 2003)

Web sites

Watch the actual restoration of a wetland after 50 years as a pasture:
www.openroad.tv/video.php?vid=399

This web page shows the effects of global warming and rising seas on coastal wetland areas:
www.coolkidsforacoolclimate.com/Causes&Effects/RisingSeaUK.htm

There are some great images of different types of wetlands on this site:
www.mbgnet.net/fresh/wetlands/index.htm

This is part of the United Kingdom's Wildfowl and Wetlands Trust site. It has useful information and quizzes on wetlands.
www.wwt.org.uk/text/301/kids_zone.html

Index